HOPE
in the
Lord

© Copyright 2023- Terry Bryant

All rights reserved. Permission is granted to copy or reprint portions for any noncommercial use, except they may not be posted online without permission.

Wyatt House books may be ordered through booksellers or by contacting:

WYATT HOUSE PUBLISHING
399 Lakeview Dr. W.
Mobile, Alabama 36695
www.wyattpublishing.com
editor@wyattpublishing.com

Because of the dynamic nature of the Internet, any web address or links contained in this book may have changed since publication and may no longer be valid.

Cover design by: Mark Wyatt

Interior design by: Mark Wyatt

ISBN 13:978-1-954798-15-1

Printed in the United States of America

HOPE in the Lord

overcoming discouragement and depression

by

Terry Bryant

Wyatt House Publishing
Mobile, Alabama

Introduction

This book is a devotional study on discouragement and depression. It includes what they are and what the Bible says about them. It is written from a spiritual and biblical point of view. This book will cover some insights the Lord has taught me from the Word and the experience of pastoring and counseling for 50 years. I desire to help individuals get encouragement from the Lord and cut off the devil's attempt to destroy a life.

Discouragement happens when we are going through a difficult situation and experiencing pressure in life, and we begin to lose the confidence that comes from being a child of God. We can start to lose our enthusiasm for life. Life often brings difficult circumstances and experiences. These experiences bring pressure and stress to us. Sometimes, the situation is so severe or prolonged that we start to feel the pressure build up inside of us to give up, hide from our problems, or run to sin to numb our emotions. We grow tired of our circumstances and start dreaming of escape. We grow tired of the battle. Discouragement can lead to depression if we do not deal with it in a Godly way.

Depression is a loss of hope, under a dark cloud of discouragement, seeing no way out of the situation, combined with a strong temptation to give up. I am not talking about having a bad day. I am discussing something that grabs your soul and mind and pulls you down. You may not want to get out of bed, or you may want to end it all. That is the description of depression that is addressed in this book.

You will see Bible characters who struggled with discouragement, and some even struggled with depression. You will see the causes and the solutions revealed in the word of God. Remember the truth that the Lord never leaves us or forsakes us.

I. We All Face Trouble

Job 14:1 Man that is born of a woman is of few days, and full of trouble. KJV

Job 5:7 For man is born for trouble, as sparks fly upward. KJV

The writer tells us we will have difficulties and hardships in these two passages. How we respond to these situations will make or break us. Listen to one of God's many promises.

Isaiah 41:13 "For I am the Lord your God, who upholds your right hand, Who says to you, 'Do not fear, I will help you.'

What a great promise! If you can grab ahold of this truth, this promise, it will serve you greatly. He said, "I will hold your hand through this storm of life. Don't be fearful. I am here to help you."

II. Everyone Hurts, Including Believers

Psalm 34:17 The righteous cry, and the Lord hears
And delivers them out of all their troubles.
18 The Lord is near to the brokenhearted
And saves those who are crushed in spirit.

It is incredible how many people around you may struggle with heaviness, and we are unaware of their pain. Many people wear a mask, pretending all is well. They are hurting inside, experiencing feelings of dismay or a sense of failure. This will result in a heavy heart. Notice several points in Psalm 34:17-18.

(A) The righteous hurt.

Ps 34:17a The righteous cry...

Being a believer does not keep you from pain and difficulties.

Ps 17b ...And the Lord delivers them out of all their troubles.

Yes, we face troubles like everyone else. And we can be affected by them like everyone else. Being a Christian does not insulate you from the trials of life. The world does not have the answer. Unbelievers stand against the struggles and hardships of life alone. But the believer has the Lord God Almighty to help him through them all.

(B) The believer can be heavy-hearted and crushed.

Ps.34:18 The Lord is near the broken-hearted...who are crushed in spirit.

But we must not stop there. We must read the rest of these verses.

v.17 "...the Lord hears...And delivers them out of ALL their trouble...v.18 The Lord is near the broken-hearted and saves them..."

Remember, the Lord hears your cries and draws near to save you. We need to trust His heart.

III. He Sees and Hears Us

Psalm 22:24 For He has not despised nor abhorred the affliction of the afflicted;
Nor has He hidden His face from him;
But when he cried to Him for help, He heard.

Even though we may sometimes feel like God is passive concerning our afflictions, David teaches that God sees every wound and suffering the believer goes through.

v.24a For He has not despised nor abhorred the affliction of the afflicted ..."

David is saying that God has not turned away from us during trouble.

v.24b ...Neither has He hidden His face from him ..."

God hasn't gone anywhere. He hasn't turned His face from our situation. Notice the next word BUT

v. 24c ...But when he cried to Him for help, He heard."

Wow! There it is again. He hears and helps. We all get stuck at times. We are tempted to give up or think God has turned His back on us. Nope! Lies! He hears and helps! Period.

IV. The Lord Helps His Afflicted

Psalms 147:2-6 shows us that God's children can suffer being outcasts, brokenhearted, and wounded. This affliction is caused by our soul's enemy, the devil.

(A) God builds and gathers.

v.2 The Lord builds up Jerusalem, He gathers the outcast of Israel.

God is building and gathering. Anytime you read the words Jerusalem and Israel in the Bible, it refers to the people of God, His children. Again, God is building up the children of God and gathering His children that have become outcasts. This world tears people down and rejects them. But our Heavenly Father does the very opposite. He gathers and builds.

(B) God heals and binds.

v.3 "He heals the brokenhearted and binds up their wounds.

Here we see the children of God experiencing heaviness of heart. Something has happened in their life to cause this sorrow. Maybe a loss of a loved one, a job, or their health. Something has happened to wound them and cause pain. A great disappointment in life can cause a massive wound. Sorrow and pain can lead to heaviness or depression if our response is incorrect.

Thankfully, this verse states that God heals. In the following few verses, God elaborates on how He heals.

(C) God counts, names, and supports.

v.4-6, He counts the number of the stars, He gives names to all of them...His understanding is infinite. The Lord supports the afflicted...

What does God knowing the number and giving names to the stars have to do with me and my situation? God, with His infinite knowledge, is aware of everything in the vast universe, and He even knows your struggles and cares, big and small. In verse 6, God states, "The Lord supports the afflicted...". That is us, His children. Our Lord can count, name stars and support us all simultaneously. How? Because He is great and mighty. He is a loving and compassionate God. He is very aware of our situation. The Lord supports the afflicted. He is coming to help. He has many answers depending on each individual's situation and needs. But be assured that the Lord supports the afflicted.

V. God Comforts Our Anxieties

Psalms 94:17-19 If the Lord had not been my help, My soul would soon have dwelt in the abode of silence. If I should say, "My foot has slipped," Your lovingkindness, O Lord, will hold me up. When my anxious thoughts multiply within me, Your consolations delight my soul.

(1) David's need for God

v17 "If the Lord has not been my help,

My soul would soon have dwelt in the abode of silence."

David was saying that if he did not have God to run to, if he did not have the Lord to call upon for help, his soul would have given up. He would have ended it all and gone to the grave.

(2) David's anxiety

v.19a When my anxious thoughts multiply within me...

David's mind started racing with confusing and perplexing thoughts about his situation and future. He became overwhelmed and panicked. That is what the devil wants us to do. He wants us to hit the panic button and let our minds think only the worst. When we believe there is no way out, our hearts and souls fall into heaviness and hopelessness.

(3) God's response

v.18 If I should say, "My foot has slipped,"

Your loving kindness, O Lord, will hold me up."

v.19b "...Your consolations delight my soul."

The word of the Lord comforted David's soul and delighted his troubled mind. Why? Because of the many promises of God caring for us. He promised He would not leave nor forsake His children. Be grateful for a God that is merciful and full of compassion. Remember, God is Love and shows mercy to those that belong to Him.

VI. God Establishes Us Through Difficulty

A. He Changes Our Thinking. (Our mind.)

Isaiah 61:3 To grant those who mourn in Zion,
Giving them a garland instead of ashes,
The oil of gladness instead of mourning,
The mantle of praise instead of a spirit of fainting.
So they will be called oaks of righteousness,
The planting of the Lord, that He may be glorified.

Isaiah describes what the Lord gives to His people who, like everyone, go through hard and difficult situations.

Isaiah 61:3a To grant those who mourn in Zion,
Giving them a garland instead of ashes,

The Lord replaces mourning hopelessness with a garland (wreath) on their head. This crown is made of flowers and describes one ruling in beauty and peace. He is giving it to His people who are mourning in Zion. Again, we hurt as everyone else does. But our Lord does something for us He does not do for the world of unbelievers and sinners. He reminds us and encourages us that we are more than conquerors through Him. We will get through whatever difficulties we face with His help.

Garlands were given to honor those who were victorious. God placing the garland on their heads is a picture of God changing their outlook and thoughts about their situation. He is reminding them that they will win in this struggle.

Revelation 5:10 You have made them to be a kingdom and priest to our God, and they will reign upon the earth.

This is talking about the 2nd coming of the Lord Jesus. In this verse, the Apostle John says (speaking of all who have chosen to follow Jesus) that the Lord is making them a kingdom where they reign on earth through one Christ Jesus. God is giving those going through hardships a garland to wear upon their heads. He is saying, "You will overcome and conquer this challenge. I've made you to reign and overcome in this life, not to be defeated." He also said, "My grace is sufficient for you." I call it the great exchange: Garland of victory and peace for ashes of mourning and heaviness. Never give up!

(B) The Lord exchanges gladness for sorrow. (Our emotions.)

Isaiah 61:3 To grant those who mourn in Zion,
Giving them a garland instead of ashes,
The oil of gladness instead of mourning,
The mantle of praise instead of a spirit of fainting.
So they will be called oaks of righteousness,
The planting of the Lord, that He may be glorified.

v.3b ...The oil of gladness instead of mourning (or sorrow) ...

Here, something has happened again to cause the heart to be sorrowful. It may be the loss of a loved one or a job, etc. Life throws many curve balls at us in our journey. It is filled with disappointments. Our Lord says that in those times, He will do something again for us. "I'll exchange sorrow for the oil of gladness." The oil represents the Holy Spirit overflowing from the top of our heads onto our clothes. It speaks of joy or gladness. How can someone be glad when sorrow comes his way? Because nothing is sorrowful in the end with Jesus.

Throughout the Bible, we read of situations where God came through. For example, when the people of Israel ran out of food and water in the wilderness, they were scared and afraid. They panicked. But Moses went to God, and the Lord worked a miracle. God told Moses to strike the rock, and water came out when he did. Then the quail flew in by the millions, and they had food. With God, difficulties, sickness, and even death do not win. Jesus is always victorious, as are we if we abide in Him. Stay strong, keep your eyes on the Lord, and never give up. We have the victory. He gives us the oil of gladness for mourning.

(C) He exchanges a spirit of fainting for a garment of praise. (Our will.)

Isaiah 61:3 To grant those who mourn in Zion,
Giving them a garland instead of ashes,
The oil of gladness instead of mourning,
The mantle of praise instead of a spirit of fainting.
So they will be called oaks of righteousness,
The planting of the Lord, that He may be glorified.

v.3c "…The mantle of praise instead of a spirit of fainting…"

Isaiah describes the believer's condition as faint, which means weak or feeble. It denotes a lamp about to go out.

They are about to give up. But God does something. He gives them a garment of praise. This is a work of the Holy Spirit in the true believer's heart. We may fall down, but God picks us up again and again. In these situations, we must choose to praise Him no matter what the circumstance looks like.

Why praise? Praise is declaring who God is. It is seeing Him and focusing on the greatness of God rather than our circumstances. This perspective will cause one to have hope and faith. We become grateful to the Lord when we praise Him. We take off weakness and feebleness when we put on the garment of praise, which is exercising faith.

(D) He Establishes Us.

v.3d "...So they will be called oaks of righteousness, the planting of the Lord..."

God answers why He is exchanging ashes for a crown, mourning for the oil of gladness, and a garment of praise for a spirit of fainting. He is establishing us as an oak planted by God in righteousness. As we mature, our steadfastness through adversity demonstrates our faith and stability to the world and glorifies God.

The key to being established is keeping our eyes on Jesus. As long as Peter kept his eyes on Jesus, he could walk on water in the storm. But he sank when he started looking at the sea and the waves. Let us keep our eyes on Jesus, who enables us to do wonders.

Bible Characters that Struggled With Discouragement and The Causes

Some causes of discouragement are fear, anxiety, exhaustion, etc. Discouragement and depression are not just modern-day issues. There are people in the bible that struggled with both of these issues. The following are some examples.

MOSES

Moses' Discouragement – Cause: Wrong Expectations

Exodus 5:22. "Then Moses returned to the Lord and said, "O Lord, why have you brought harm to this people? Why did You ever send me?"

God had commanded Moses to go to Pharaoh and demand that he set God's people free. Instead, Pharaoh increased their suffering. Then the people of Israel blamed Moses for Pharoah's actions. Moses was feeling down and discouraged about everything that was happening. He didn't envision circumstances developing the way they did. All these things discouraged Moses. Many times, unmet expectations will cause disappointment, and disappointment will lead to discouragement. Moses felt a sense of failure and even questioned God.

Exodus 5:22 … "Oh Lord…why have You brought harm to this people?"

If we are not careful, we will blame God if things don't turn out as we expected. God told Moses that Pharaoh would not listen at first, but he would in the end. Moses' expectations were out of line with what God had said, which caused Moses to ask God the second question.

Exodus 5:22 ... "O Lord... Why did You ever send me?"

Because Moses' expectations were out of line, he felt like a failure. Be patient with God's timing. His ways are not our ways.

ISRAEL

Israel's Discouragement – Cause: Lack of Provision

Exodus 17 records the story of the children of Israel in the wilderness. They had been rescued from Egyptian bondage and followed Moses, and Moses was following the Lord through the wilderness. They did not have water and got discouraged. They blamed Moses and the Lord for their situation. They said that God led them into the wilderness to die.

Exodus 17:1b ...camped at Rephidim, and there was no water for the people to drink.

Exodus 17:3b ... "Why, now, have you brought us up from Egypt, to kill us and our children and our livestock with thirst?"

At some point, everyone faces a situation where they are in need. The enemy will use this opportunity to attack you with discouragement and depression. The devil will tell you God will abandon you, and you will never make it. This is not true. God saw their situation and told Moses to take the rod (staff) in his hand and strike the rock. When Moses obeyed the Lord, water came forth from the rock.

Exodus 17:6a "Behold, I will stand before you there on the rock at Horeb; and you shall strike the rock, and water will come out of it, that the people may drink..."

When Moses had needs, he responded differently than the people. He sought the Lord's help. And he obeyed the Lord's directions. Listen to God's response to Moses. Go to the rock at Horeb. There I'll be standing on the rock.

v.6 "Behold I will stand before you there on the rock..."

The Lord was present with them. They didn't recognize and acknowledge Him. But Moses did, and God worked a miracle, one of many. He did not save us to destroy us because He has a plan for us. We must keep our focus on His sufficiency rather than on our lack. He will provide.

ELIJAH

Elijah's Discouragement – Cause: Physical, Emotional, and Spiritual Exhaustion

Elijah was a great prophet of God. During his service to God, we find him discouraged next to a stream and, later, in a cave. How do you go from serving God powerfully with a great victory over the false prophets of Baal, even calling fire down from heaven, to being in a cave discouraged? (The answer is revealed as we see what happened to Elijah, which we address in detail in the following paragraphs.) Elijah served God faithfully to the point of physical, emotional, and spiritual exhaustion. The exhaustion was so great that he wanted to die. You can find yourself going quickly from the mountaintop of victory to the valley of discouragement. This is why Jesus, after ministering to thousands, departed to pray. He knew He needed a time of rest and renewal.

Believe it or not, physical and emotional exhaustion can cause someone to become discouraged and even depressed. When a person is under stress, and that stress empties them, they hit the wall emotionally and physically. They feel drained of everything. In these situations, their system shuts down, and depression can set in. Elijah experienced such discouragement and depression. Let us get into the details of Elijah's case and the solution.

1 Kings 19:3-4 "And he was afraid and arose and ran for his life…he himself went a day's journey into the wilderness and came and sat down under a juniper tree, and he requested for himself that he might die…"

Elijah was having a terrible day. What's the backstory? Israel had fallen into sin under the leadership of King Ahab and his wife, Jezebel. The country had turned to Baal worship because of Jezebel's influence. God told Elijah to go before the king and prophesy, "A drought is coming to Israel, and it will not rain until I say so." Elijah also challenged the false prophets of Baal, killing 450 of them in the end. Jezebel was furious and threatened to kill Elijah. He became fearful and fled to the wilderness. He ran to the point of exhaustion and wanted to die. After running so far, he got down emotionally and became depressed. He hit that emotional and physical wall and was spent. How do you know? In 1 Kings 19:5-8, we see a pattern to help us understand Elijah's situation.

v.5a He lay down and slept under a juniper tree…

He was tired and exhausted. Notice what the angel from the Lord said.

v5b …and there was an angel touching him and said to him, "Arise, eat."

Then Elijah fell back to sleep. He was totally exhausted and weak from hunger. Remember, there had been a drought for six months. He needed a fresh touch from God, food, and rest. The answer to Elijah's depression was three-fold:

(1) A spiritual touch from heaven.

(2) Rest.

(3) Food - both physical and spiritual.

The result was

v.8 ...(he) went in the strength of that food forty days and forty nights...

Elijah was renewed and refreshed. He overcame the feeling of depression and went on to serve the Lord mightily. With the Lord, there is always hope and victory over our struggles. All we need is a fresh touch from heaven, some spiritual food, and a little rest. After that, we are up and running again, beloved.

DAVID

David's Discouragement – Cause: Sin

Psalm 32: 3 When I kept silent about my sin, my body wasted away
Through my groaning all day long.
4 For day and night Your hand was heavy upon me; My vitality was drained away as with the fever heat of summer. Selah.

Psalm 32 covers some consequences of David's affair with Bathsheba.

(1) God's hand is heavy on David

This is the conviction of the Holy Spirit on David because of his sin. When we sin against God in open disobedience, the heavy conviction of God Almighty will come down upon us. The weight of guilt is emotionally draining, which leads us to discouragement and despair about our failures.

(2) There is a grieving process.

When we are under conviction from God because of sin, we grieve the loss of fellowship with God our Father. We experience a loss of power and victory because we are out of fellowship with God. This is the point where despair and depression can set in. David felt as if he was wasting away. He was getting weaker and found himself crying day and night. This is a picture of a broken man.

(3) But listen to how David was restored

Psalm 32:1 How blessed is he whose transgression is forgiven...

Psalm 32:5 I acknowledged my sin to You,
And my iniquity I did not hide;
I said, "I will confess my transgressions to the Lord";
And You forgave the guilt of my sin. Selah.

Those verses show us the way out of the despair that comes from our sinful behavior. To recover, we cannot hide our sin. We acknowledge and confess it to the Lord. And He will forgive and restore us. Joy will replace heaviness. It is much easier to obey.

PETER

Peter's Discouragement. Cause: Sin

Peter fell into heavy despair after he denied Jesus. And after Jesus' death, he continued in despair.

Luke 22:61-62 The Lord turned and looked at Peter. And Peter remembered the word of the Lord, how He had told him, "Before a rooster crows today, you will deny Me three times." 62 And he went out and wept bitterly.

I can't imagine how Peter felt when Jesus turned and looked at him right as he denied the Lord. We know the bible says Peter went back to fishing. He gave up and quit because he was so disappointed in himself. He thought Jesus was done with him. This is a typical scene in every believer who has experienced failure. They also feel that God cannot use them. They tend to be so discouraged that they give up. This is where the enemy will severely attack you and continuously remind you of your failure. He will lie to us and say that God can no longer use us. But no! Just like Jesus was not finished with Peter, God is not finished with us. After the resurrection, Jesus found Peter and reassured him that God wasn't finished with him. Peter became one of the strongest preachers of Jesus and the resurrection. Thousands were saved at Pentecost and brought into the kingdom of God through his preaching. Thankfully our Lord is full of mercy and grace and can restore you.

JUDAS

Judas' Discouragement and Depression. Cause: Sin

Now let us look at a sad story in the Bible of a character who got overwhelmed by depression and chose to end his life. He was not a true believer. He was one in name only. I am speaking of Judas, who betrayed Jesus for 30 pieces of silver.

Matthew 27:3 Then when Judas, who had betrayed Him, saw that He (Jesus) had been condemned, he felt remorse (he felt terrible, but not repentant) and returned the thirty pieces of silver to the chief priests and elders.

Judas was a man who loved money rather than God. He sold out the Son of God for 30 pieces of silver. His heart was not true to Jesus. Notice v.4

Matthew 27:4 ... "I have sinned by betraying innocent blood." But they said, "What is that to us?" See to that yourself."

Judas realized his betrayal was going to bring about the death of Jesus. He felt remorse and threw the money at the elders. He knew Jesus was innocent. Notice the end of Judas' story.

v.5 ...and departed; and he went away and hanged himself.

Judas was overwhelmed with remorse and guilt. Depressed and hopeless, he made a terrible decision. He chose to end his life. Suicide is never the answer. There is no difference between Peter's denial of Jesus and Judas' betrayal of Jesus. Both were sins. Even though the sins may not differ, how we respond to our sins may vary significantly. One chose to be restored to the Lord (Peter). The other (Judas) decided to run away from the Lord, sink into depression, and end his life—two completely different responses. Way too many people give up and end their life when there is still hope, forgiveness, and restoration available. Look and learn from these men. Choose to respond like Peter after your sin.

JONAH

Jonah's Discouragement and Depression – Cause: Sin – Disobedience, Disappointment, and Anger

Despair can come when life throws you a curve. Life has many unexpected events. Some of which can floor you emotionally. This happened to Jonah when he held on to expectations that were not fulfilled. God commissioned Jonah to deliver a message to Nineveh, which was one of certain judgment. But when the people of Nineveh heard the message, they repented. Because of their response, God relented and spared them. This angered the prophet Jonah and started a spiral decline in his walk. Let us look closer at Jonah and his story.

(1) God speaks

Jonah 1:1-2 The word of the Lord came to Jonah, the son of Amittai saying, 2 "Arise, go to Nineveh the great city and cry against it, for their wickedness has come up before Me."

God was very clear in what He told Jonah. Jonah didn't have to think about it. Just do it. How does a Christian know what God requires of us if we don't read and study the word of God? They don't. That's a dangerous place to live.

(2) Jonah refused to obey

Jonah 1:3 But Jonah rose up to flee to Tarshish from the presence of the Lord...

This verse shows Jonah did not want to follow the Lord's command. He fled in the other direction. He was deeply prejudiced against the Ninevites because of their cruelty against his people. Therefore, he ran. Jonah was concerned that God would show Nineveh mercy.

Jonah 4:2 And he prayed to the Lord and said, "Please Lord, was not this what I said while I was still in my own country? Therefore, in order to forestall this I fled to Tarshish, for I knew that Thou art a gracious and compassionate God, slow to anger and abundant in lovingkindness, and one who relents concerning calamity.

A word to the believer: You cannot outrun God.

(3) We can never escape the Lord

This is seen in Psalm 139:7-10

7 Where can I go from Your Spirit?
Or where can I flee from Your presence?
8 If I ascend to heaven, You are there;
If I make my bed in Sheol, behold, You are there.
9 If I take the wings of the dawn,
If I dwell in the remotest part of the sea,

10 Even there Your hand will lead me,
And Your right hand will lay hold of me.

No truer words were ever written by the Psalmist. We cannot get away from the Lord.

(4) Disobeying the Lord has consequences

Consequences are sometimes seen and sometimes unseen. For instance, situations turn against us, or things don't go as planned. Some consequences are unseen; depression, despair, heaviness, anxiety, etc. Jonah's despair was brought on by his disobedience. God, in His sovereignty, knew of Jonah's choice to rebel and was already ahead of him. God decided Jonah needed some time to think about his choices and brought some seen and unseen consequences down on Jonah.

Jonah 1:17 And the Lord appointed a great fish to swallow Jonah, and Jonah was in the stomach of the fish three days and three nights.

For three days and three nights, Jonah sat and thought about his decision in the belly of a fish. This experience caused him to faint away inwardly.

(5) In our despair, we need to remember the Lord.

Jonah 2:7 While I was fainting away,
I remembered the Lord,
And my prayer came to You...

Jonah came to his senses in the belly of the fish and remembered the Lord, and returned to Him. He was fainting away. He was giving up hope. He was in despair. Then he remembered the Lord. Praise God! He is the God of second chances.

Jonah repented, and God delivered him. Then Jonah went to Nineveh and preached God's message. The people repented and turned to God. Therefore, the Lord changed His mind and spared the people of Nineveh. Our foolish choices can be the reason for our despair and can affect others. Let us learn from Jonah and choose to obey and follow the Lord.

(6) Disappointment and Anger

The city heard Jonah's message and repented, both great and small.

God showed mercy to Nineveh and spared them. This angered Jonah. He was disappointed that God did not judge them for their sins.

Jonah 3:10 When God saw their deeds, that they turned from their wicked way, then God relented concerning the calamity which He had declared He would bring upon them. And He did not do it.
4:1 But it greatly displeased Jonah, and he became angry.

Unmet expectations can cause disappointment. Disappointment will lead to anger. If we do not respond to anger and disappointment correctly, they lead us to a dark pit of despair and discouragement.

4:3 "Therefore now, O Lord, please take my life from me, for death is better to me than life."

We know that Jonah eventually overcame his anger and disappointment because he is the one telling the story. Jonah revealed all of his flaws and weaknesses when he wrote the book. He was transparent with God and with us. The first step to getting help from God is being honest and transparent about our sins, faults, and weaknesses.

James 5:16 Confess your trespasses to one another, and pray for one another, that you may be healed.

To avoid disappointment and anger, we must lay down our expectations regarding God and our circumstances. Remember, Jesus said, "Not my will Lord but Thine be done." Let God be God in your situation and accomplish His will in you.

JEREMIAH

Jeremiah's Discouragement and Depression – Cause: Loneliness, Rejection, Abuse, and Suffering

Jeremiah was known as the weeping prophet. He was called by God and chosen to speak a prophetic message. He was not allowed to marry or have children. His message was of the coming destruction of Israel, but the people of God rejected it. Jeremiah suffered heavy rejection and loneliness throughout his ministry and was eventually imprisoned. He was a faithful servant of God, yet he struggled with despair.

Jeremiah 20:14,18 Cursed be the day when I was born...Why did I ever come forth from the womb to look on trouble and sorrow, so that my days have been spent in shame (rejection)?

I can't imagine receiving an assignment from God that required me to endure such abuse, being locked up and beaten.

Jeremiah 37:15-16 The officials were angry at Jeremiah and beat him, and they put him in jail...For Jeremiah had come into the dungeon, that is, the vaulted cell; and Jeremiah stayed there many days.

They did not like the message of repentance and the fact that Babylon would take them into captivity; therefore, they abused Jeremiah. Wow! What a lonely life of suffering. It reminds me of Jesus, a man of sorrow. Even though Jeremiah struggled with despair, he never gave up. He stayed faithful and remembered the promise God gave him and Israel.

Jeremiah 29:11 For I know the plans that I have for you, declares the Lord, plans for welfare (prosperity) and not for calamity to give you a future and a hope.

God chastened Israel for sin and disobedience by sending them into Babylonian captivity. He never intended to destroy them but to discipline them. He responded like a father would to an unruly child and used the ROD of correction. Jeremiah held on to the promise in verse 11. This was God reaching out to Jeremiah in his day of despair. Sometimes, we need a word from God to get us out of the valley of despair. We believers should hold on to the promise in verse 11 and keep the faith.

JOB

Job's Discouragement and Depression – Cause: The Test of Trials

Let us look deep into the life of Job and his struggle with adversity and suffering. How did he respond? What lessons can we learn to avoid falling into despair and depression? You will observe that Job endured several different attacks from the devil. Each attack was designed to break Job down and cause him to give up. Now we will study the many tests that Job had to endure.

(A) First Trial – Loss of wealth and substance

Job 1:13-15 Now it happened on the day…that a messenger came to Job and said, "The oxen were plowing and the donkeys feeding beside them, 15 and the Sabeans attacked and took them…"

v16 While he was still speaking (the first servant telling of the bad news), another also came and said, "The fire of God fell from heaven and burned up the sheep and the servants…"

The same day Job lost his oxen and donkeys, lightning struck and started a fire that consumed his sheep and servants. That's not all.

v17 While he was still speaking, another also came and said, "The Chaldeans formed three bands and made a raid on the camels and took them and slew the servants..."

Job lost all of this in one day. Bad news after bad news. How did Job respond?

Job 1:21 He said,
"Naked I came from my mother's womb,
And naked I shall return there.
The Lord gave and the Lord has taken away.
Blessed be the name of the Lord."

Job had a strong walk with God and had tremendous knowledge and understanding. He did not look at life through his own selfish eyes and make everything about him. Job had a higher purpose for his life. He lived for God's glory. Beloved, things come and things go in life. But let us always bless the name of the Lord and live for Him! Job passed the first test.

(B) Second Trial - Loss of loved ones

In this trial, we see a tragic loss, the death of Job's children. One cannot imagine how painful it is to lose a child you love. It breaks the heart of a parent. Unfortunately, I have experienced the loss of a child. The pain was deep and indescribable. Notice how Job responded.

Job 1:18-20,22 While he was still speaking (the servant bringing bad news), another also came and said, "Your sons and your daughters were eating and drinking wine in their oldest brother's house, and behold, a great wind came from across the wilderness and struck the four corners of the house, and it fell on the young people and they died..." Then Job arose and tore his robe (in grief) and shaved his head and he fell to the ground and worshiped.

Through all this, Job did not sin or blame God. I am astonished at Job's response. When a parent loses a child, their life is torn to pieces. The only way they can keep from losing it is to fall on their face and cry out to God. During such a trial, God has to hold us together because we cannot do that in our own power. But when you turn to Him, He will hold you with His right hand so you do not slip and stumble. Rather than fall into despair and depression, Job chose to fall on his face before God and worship Him. And that is how Job overcame the tragedy of losing His children. Job passed the test.

He also said:

Job 1:21b "The Lord gave and the Lord has taken away. Blessed be the name of the Lord."

Job could endure because of his faith, understanding of life, and the strength the Lord gave him in the midst of adversity. I hope and pray you never lose a child. But if you do, remember Job's response.

It helped me immensely. The Lord's strength and grace can heal the brokenhearted. This is the most personal part of the book for me. I still miss my son to this day. When I remember that day, I remember the pain. But I also remember the Lord's comfort and strength. I can say God's grace is sufficient. Praise His name.

(C) Third Trial – Physical Infirmity

Job 2:7-8 Then Satan went out from the presence of the Lord and smote Job with sore boils from the sole of his foot to the crown of his head. 8 And he (Job) took a potsherd to scrape himself while he was sitting among the ashes.

No one knows the kind of suffering Job went through unless they have been through severe physical suffering. During this time, Satan's attack on Job was an effort to break him. But Job remained faithful and refused to turn on the Lord.

James 5:11 We count those blessed who endured. You have heard of the endurance of Job and have seen the outcome of the Lord's dealings, that the Lord is full of compassion and is merciful.

The early notion about physical suffering was that the righteous are healthy and the wicked are sickly and unhealthy. Job proved this doctrine false. God said Job was the most righteous man to walk the earth at that time. Yet, he had to endure physical sickness and pain. The devil was trying to break Job down with the loss of wealth and things. Then it was the loss of loved ones. Now his attack is inflicting physical suffering. Through it all, Job remained faithful and would not curse God. Beloved, God's grace is sufficient, and His mercy endures forever. That is the message of James 5:11. Do not give up when you go through sickness and suffering. The Lord has not forsaken you.

(D) Fourth Trial – Family trial

Look at how Job's wife responded to his adversity.

Job 2:9 Then his wife said to him, "Do you still hold fast your integrity? Curse God and die!"

What was she thinking? I know she saw Job's suffering and felt compassion for him. But this was not good advice. God was testing Job, and that is why he was experiencing adversity. God was revealing Job's heart to all creation. Job loved and served God because of who He was, not because of the blessings God could give him. It is hard enough to suffer, but to suffer alone is extremely difficult—Notice Job's response.

Job 2:10 But he said to her, "You speak as one of the foolish women speaks. Shall we indeed accept good from God and not accept adversity?" In all this Job did not sin with his lips.

Job had knowledge and understanding that others did not possess on that day. He is an example to us all. Understand that adversity is always a test for us. The way that we overcome physical adversity is to believe God is in control and will get us through any test/trial we face.

(E) Fifth trial – Judgment of Others

Job's wife gave him bad advice, and his friends judged him wrongly.

Job 2:11 Now when Job's three friends heard of all this adversity that had come upon him, they came...

v13 Then they sat down on the ground with him for seven days and seven nights with no one speaking a word to him, for they saw that his pain was very great.

But then the Bible states they began to accuse Job of iniquities and said his sin caused the adversity.

Job 22:5 Is not your wickedness great,
And your iniquities without end?

This verse is from the mouth of one of Job's friends. You know the old saying, "With friends like these, who needs enemies." Job had lost wealth, children, health, and his wife's support. Then his friends turned on him. In all this, Job still did not sin against God and curse Him. How did Job ultimately respond to his friends?

Job 42:10 The Lord restored the fortunes of Job WHEN HE PRAYED for his friends, and the Lord increased all that Job had twofold.

He PRAYED for them. They accused Job of being wicked and sinful as the reason for his suffering. But Job PRAYED for them. This man is an excellent example to us. He is a type and shadow of Jesus, the man of suffering! Listen, bad things can come upon righteous people. The question is, how will we respond? We can crumble in despair and anxiety or stand firm in the Lord's strength. Stand strong and endure.

JESUS

Jesus Overcoming Anxiety – Cause: The Sufferings of the Cross

As we conclude our study on despair and suffering, we must look at the Lord Jesus.

He was a man of suffering. He was rejected, betrayed, and abandoned by his disciples. He suffered emotionally and physically. Yet, like Job of the Old Testament, Jesus never let despair or discouragement overcome Him, even under extreme pressure. He endured all trials and stayed faithful to His Heavenly Father. But we must be honest; Jesus had an incident in the garden where the pressure was extremely intense. Jesus saw the suffering coming and sweated great drops of blood as His body experienced the anxiety and dread of the cross. Jesus even asked the Father if He had to drink this bitter cup. He asked if there was another way. We all know the cup represents the sufferings of the cross.

Notice how Jesus responded in the garden.

Mark 14:34-35 And He said to them, "My soul is deeply grieved to the point of death; remain here and keep watch." 35 And He went a little beyond them, and fell to the ground and began to pray that if it were possible, the hour might pass Him by. (In other words, He wouldn't have to suffer and die on the cross.)

Notice His response in the next verse.

v36 "And He was saying, Abba! Father! All things are possible for You; remove this cup from Me; yet not what I will, but what You will."

The Bible says He endured the cross for His Father and for our sakes so we might be redeemed. Hallelujah! He experienced anxiety and dread. But He overcame them by submitting to the will of God and trusting His Heavenly Father.

1 Peter 2:23 and while being reviled, He did not revile in return; while suffering, He uttered no threats, but kept entrusting Himself to Him who judges righteously.

Summary of Bible Characters

Let's review the characters and their issues with despair and notice what they did to get through it.

(1) Moses

Cause: circumstances didn't go as he expected.

Effect: Disappointment brought despair.

Solution: Be patient and trust God.

Result: Moses learned to trust God through all difficulties.

(2) Israel

Cause: Lack of provision

Effect: Panic and despair.

Solution: Moses sought the Lord and obeyed His instructions.

Result: Israel learned to trust the leader God gave them.

(3) Elijah

Cause: Exhausted physically and spiritually.

Effect: Fear, Despair, and Isolation

Solution: Rest and food (including spiritual food).

Result: God restored Elijah's physical and spiritual strength.

(4) David, Peter, and Jonah

Cause: Sin

Effect: Broken fellowship with God, which leads to despair.

Answer: Confession and repentance; then God will restore you and return the joy of your salvation.

Result: God restored David to his former greatness. God made Peter stronger than before, and he became God's mouthpiece at Pentecost. Jonah learned to obey God, resulting in Nineveh's salvation and a book of the Bible that has encouraged millions.

(5) Jeremiah

Cause: Rejection

Effect: Loneliness and despair.

Answer: Never gave up. He stayed strong by standing on God's promise(s).

Result: Jeremiah became one of God's greatest prophets.

(6) Job

Cause: Multiple adversities and trials

Effect: Suffering

Answer: Job trusted. Therefore, he never broke.

Job 13:15a Though he slay me, yet will I trust in him… KJV

Result: God demonstrated to Satan and the world that He had a man that would not break under pressure.

(7) Jesus

Cause: Multiple adversities and trials.

Effect: Much suffering.

Answer: He stayed committed to God.

Luke 22:42b …not My will, but Thine be done.

1 Peter 2:23b …kept entrusting Himself to Him who judges righteously;

Result: God elevated His name above all names. He is our ultimate example of how to deal with difficulties.

This is a summary of the amazing bible characters and their faith. They struggle with despair, anxiety, and depression, yet they came out victoriously. They gave us an example that we are more than conquerors with the Lord.

Epilogue

Passages of encouragement

This epilogue provides some passages and thoughts of encouragement to get you through times of difficulty.

Philippians 4:6-7 Be anxious for nothing, but in everything by prayer and supplication with thanksgiving let your requests be made known to God. 7 And the peace of God, which surpasses all comprehension, will guard your hearts and your minds in Christ Jesus.

This is a powerful verse of comfort when faced with a situation that would cause the heart and mind to be troubled. Notice it started with anxiety but ended with God's peace guarding the heart and mind. How exactly does that work?

(1) Always pray and petition God about the situation.

If there is anxiety, there is a situation. God instructs us that we are to pray to Him in everything and that His peace will guard us. Do not try to figure it out without God's presence and wisdom. Run to God, pray, listen, trust, and obey.

(2) Pray with thanksgiving.

Thanking God ahead of time is a sign of faith. We must have faith to walk with God.

Hebrews 11:6 And without faith it is impossible to please Him, for he who comes to God must believe that He is and that He is a rewarder of those who seek Him.

We exercise our faith in God by seeking Him in prayer, petition, and thanksgiving. He promises to reward us when we walk in faith. What is the reward?

(3) Peace of God

What is the result of trusting Him? Peace and safety for our hearts and mind through difficult situations. Our prayer is directed to our heavenly Father because He is the only one that can help us in times of difficulty. Even before the answer reaches us, the peace of God that surpasses all comprehension will guard our hearts and minds. No child of God has to walk around alone with fear and anxiety. Praise His name! You can walk in peace, trusting the Lord.

Isaiah 41:10 'Do not fear, for I am with you; Do not anxiously look about you, for I am your God. I will strengthen you, surely I will help you, Surely I will uphold you with My righteous right hand.'

In Isaiah 41:10, God tells us not to fear or be afraid. How can a person stop being afraid?

(1) God says do not be afraid.

Isaiah 41:10 "Do not fear...Do not be anxious..."

If we're struggling with fear, something is going on that is causing the fear. He sees the situation and instructs us, "Don't be afraid!" Why?

(2) I AM with you.

v.10 "Do not fear, for I am with you;
Do not anxiously look about you, for I am your God..."

It is one thing to face a troubling situation alone. It is another thing to face it with God. How we handle our situation will change once we understand that we are never alone and that He will never forsake us.

Hebrews 13:5b for He Himself has said, "I will never desert you, nor will I ever forsake you,"...

The difficulty we face may not change right away. What does change is that our faith becomes strong when we recognize God's presence with us. Sometimes as we change, our situation changes. If the problem does not change, we learn to endure it.

You can face anything with God. Remember, He is the great I AM. "I AM THAT I AM." What does that mean? "I AM the answer to every need you have. I AM whatever you need."

(3) God will strengthen you.

v.10 "...I will strengthen you, surely I will help you, Surely I will uphold you..."

We must stop focusing on the problem and look to the Lord our strength. When faced with something fearful, one will often lose strength and weaken in the knees. But God says, "Don't be afraid; I am going to give you strength for those weak knees. I will help you and hold you up during this time." What an encouraging passage from God's word. Keep your eyes on God and His provision.

Joshua 1:9 Have I not commanded you? Be strong and courageous! Do not tremble or be dismayed, for the Lord your God is with you wherever you go.

When Israel was about to enter Canaan, God gave them this command through Joshua. At this point in the scriptures, Moses, who had passed away, had led the people of Israel out of Egypt and through the wilderness. Moses sent spies to observe the land, and they saw giants there. All but two of the spies were afraid and told Israel they could not defeat their enemies. The spies said the giants were too big and Israel too small. Joshua and Caleb were the two who were not afraid. After Moses died and Joshua became the leader of Israel. Now they are looking to take the promised land from the enemy. That is when God reminded Joshua of this command.

(1) Be Strong and courageous.

When faced with a situation that is much bigger than you, God encourages you to be strong and fearless at that moment. We are to stand in faith, trusting His promise.

(2) Don't tremble.

Do not be shaken in these moments. Do not be dismayed. Do not be confused. It is easy to look at the size of the problem and our smallness and be shaken. But God instructs us how to face these situations.

(3) The Lord your God is with you wherever you go.

Whatever situation we face, no matter how huge or impossible, we do not fear because the Lord is with us. The enemy was bigger than Joshua but not bigger than the Lord our God. Therefore, we must remember that the Lord is with us in every situation and circumstance.

Romans 15:13 Now may the God of hope fill you with all joy and peace in believing, so that you will abound in hope by the power of the Holy Spirit.

Romans 15:13 teaches us how to maintain hope in life.

(1) God is the God of hope.

The Lord is described in this verse as a God of Hope. Nothing is impossible with the Lord our God. There is always hope that He will deliver, heal, and help you. He is the God of Hope!

(2) He fills you with joy and peace.

Notice the results of having hope in your life. It results in joy and peace. There is no fear when an individual has hope, joy, and peace. You are at peace. Why? Because He fills your life with confidence, and He cannot be shaken.

(3) You trust in the Lord.

v.13 "...fill you with joy and peace in BELIEVING..."

You are trusting God in all situations. Whatever you face, you can walk in faith because you believe in God and stand upon His word.

Where does this Hope come from?

(4) Hope is coming from the Holy Spirit.

v.13 "...so that you will abound in hope by the Holy Spirit."

Interestingly, hope is the byproduct of faith, and faith is a fruit of the Spirit.

Galatians 5:22 But the fruit of the Spirit is...faithfulness...

Trusting God produces hope, and hope produces joy and peace. Faith will rise as we learn to walk in the power of the Holy Spirit. God will fill us with hope, joy, and peace as we trust Him. Now that is how we live victoriously.

Psalm 94:18-19 If I should say, "My foot has slipped,"
Your lovingkindness, O Lord, will hold me up.
19 When my anxious thoughts multiply within me,
Your consolations delight my soul.

Psalms 94:18-19 gives us some encouraging words about the God who cares for us.

(1) The Psalmist slipped and stumbled.

This could mean he almost fell spiritually, or it may mean he did fall spiritually. In life, the devil puts obstacles in front of us, trying to cause us to fall. If we are careful in how we walk, we can avoid stumbling. Even though the enemy is against us, the Lord is for us. "It was the Lord that held me up." The Lord's lovingkindness motivated Him to deal with David as a father does His son. Even if we stumble, He still loves us and will hold us up.

When anyone experiences a stumble or a fall, guilt and shame can cause the believer to doubt that God is still for him. But this passage states that He is there and holding you up, even though your feelings contradict the word of God. Therefore, we have to override our feelings, grab hold of the word in faith, and believe and know that no matter if we fall or what we feel, He is still there and has hold of us in love.

(2) God consoled him.

The word consolation means "the comfort received by a person after a loss or disappointment." In this verse, God comforts us after our loss or disappointment. He is encouraging us that all is not lost. God is the God of a second chance. The Lord's words are a delight to the soul that is wounded by loss and failure. Let His Word console your soul today.

Isaiah 9:6 ... And His name will be called Wonderful Counselor...

Psalm 55:22 Cast your burden upon the Lord and He will sustain you;
He will never allow the righteous to be shaken.

Life can be burdensome at times. This psalm gives us the steps to take when we're heavily burdened.

(1) Put the things weighing you down on the Lord.

Things often arise in your life that are too difficult to carry. The psalmist says to cast them upon the Lord. His shoulders are strong enough to carry your burdens. If the Lord Jesus can take the heavy burden of the cross and the sin of the world after being beaten all night, His shoulders are strong enough to carry your troubles, cares, and burdens.

1 Peter 5:7 casting all your anxiety on Him, because He cares for you.

(2) He will sustain you.

You have to deal with the issues even as you cast

your burden upon the Lord. The Lord with strengthen you as you work through each situation. He will carry you and sustain you.

(3) He gives a promise.

v.22 ...He will never allow the righteous to be shaken.

The promise is that you will not be shaken if you cast your burdens upon the Lord. You will get through the ordeal. I can testify to the fact that this verse is true. I have often come to the end of myself, cried out to Him, and put my heavy burden upon the Lord. I got to see Him come through time and time again. Why? He is faithful.

Concluding thought: Never give up. God will encourage and establish you. He will turn this to your good and help you and those around you.

ABOUT THE AUTHOR

Terry Bryant has been a minister of the Gospel of Jesus Christ for 50 years. He was saved at the age of 18. He married Sherry in 1975 and they are the proud parents of 11 children. He has served as youth minister, and pastored several churches. He also served 6 years as a missionary in Haiti. Terry was in country when the Haitian government was overthrown and the whole country erupted in killings and chaos. He has been a street evangelist, and carried a 10 foot cross through the state of Alabama. He preached Resurrection rallies on all the major and minor college campuses, and has been a national conference speaker. Dr Fred Wolfe was his mentor throughout his ministry. There have been several Godly individuals that have impacted his life, including Jack Taylor, Peter Lord, Leonard Ravenhill, James Robinson, and Ms. Bertha Smith. His desire now is to write books and share God's insights with the next generation.

He is also the author of *Standing Firm in the Evil Day*, available from online retailers and Wyatt House Publishing.

You have a story.
We want to publish it.

Everyone has as a story to tell. It might be about something you know how to do, or what has happened in your life, or it may be a thrilling, or romantic, or intriguing, or heartwarming, or suspenseful story, starring a cast of characters that have been swimming around in your imagination.

And at Wyatt House Publishing, we can get your story onto the pages of a book just like the one you are holding in your hand. With professional interior design and a custom, professionally designed cover built just for you from the start, you can finally see your dream of being an author become reality. Then, you will see your book listed with retailers all over the world as people are able to buy your book from wherever they are and have it delivered to their home or their e-reader.

So what are you waiting for? This is your time.

visit us at
www.wyattpublishing.com

for details on how to get started becoming a published author right away.